THE BREAD GAME

REVISED EDITION

MONEY

*. . . there is the theory of raising funds from foundations
. . . and there is the reality*

Library of Congress Cataloging in Publication Data
Main entry under title:

The Bread game.

"A joint venture of the Regional Young Adult Project
and Pacific Change, San Francisco, California."
    1. Fund raising. 2. Proposal writing in the
social sciences. I. Allen, Herb, ed. II. Abrahams,
Peter D. III. Regional Young Adult Project.
IV. Pacific Change (Organization)
HV41.B656 1974   361.7'3   74-3094
ISBN 0-912078-40-5

This handbook is designed to self-destruct when new data is available.
You are therefore invited to feed your thoughts and comments into the
hopper for revision and expansion of *The Bread Game*. Let us hear
from you!

Additional copies of *The Bread Game* may be ordered at $2.95 from
Glide Publications, 330 Ellis Street, San Francisco, Ca. 94102. Please
include $.50 postage and handling per copy ordered plus an additional
$.10 per copy sales tax if you order in the state of California. Payment
must accompany order.

First Edition 1973
Revised Edition 1974

CONTRIBUTORS

Peter D. Abrahams
Herb Allen
Elliott Buchdruker
JoAnn Silverstein
Tom Silk
Ida Strickland

EDITOR

Herb Allen, Director
Regional Young Adult Project

A JOINT VENTURE OF

Regional Young Adult Project
Pacific Change

San Francisco, California

**GRATEFUL ACKNOWLEDGMENTS
FOR MAKING THIS BOOK POSSIBLE**

Stern Fund, New York

D.J.B. Foundation, New York

Urban Young Adult Action

Cover & Text Design by
SHARPSHOOTER STUDIOS

CONTENTS

1

The

Bread Game

The Rules

If you are about to enter into the world of "grantmanship," the following pages will give you some ideas about the nature and feeding habits of the beast known as *foundations.* This creature comes in all shapes and sizes, and it is estimated that the U.S. abounds with a population of more than 26,000 of them. The ability and the willingness of the foundation beast to fund programs and projects are controlled by many factors which include everything from the animal known as "super-beast" (the government in general, and Internal Revenue Service in particular) to the wishes and quirks of the donors, boards of directors, executive staff and all the other parts that make up the beast. It will be helpful for you to remember that foundations are made up of mammals known as human beings. Their characteristics are not unlike yours: they have their problems, hopes, likes, dislikes, prejudices, goals, whims, concerns, and responsibilities, and like the rest of us they like to get their jollies.

The foundation beast tends to be shy and retiring when it comes to controversy, social change, risk and all those conditions which may tend to upset the status quo. While there does exist a certain breed of foundation beast willing to move on the broad front of social change, these tend to be few and far between. Too many have withdrawn into their wombs where they can feed themselves on the warm feelings generated by funding, safe, non-controversial enterprises. This particular form of the beast lacks a social consciousness and only by special nurture and educational training will it be able to awaken a new sense of how it might better use its talents and assets. If it can be educated to overcome its fear of the unknown, it can perhaps be led out into the world of reality and take its place with the new liberated breed.

Because of the imposing size and appearance of the foundation beast, many humans approach timidly: poorly prepared, uninformed. As a result they are generally intimidated by the scene. But if you do your homework and learn all that you can about any one of the beasts with which you would like to develop a "granting" relationship, you will soon discover that the beast can be tamed and that a good relationship can be established.

To do this, it is essential to be armed with the following information:

1. A well-written presentation.

2. Research about foundations which have some history of interest in the field covered by the presentation.

3. A track record which demonstrates your ability to implement the program.

4. Where you raised the initial bread from: friends, relatives, community, individuals, other organizations, whatever.

5. *The financial capacity of the foundation—average size of grants they make.*
6. *The relationship that may exist between the grant seeker and the foundation.*
7. *Last but not least, awareness of the need for proper timing and a personal interview. Be perseverent even if first efforts fail!*

Our foundation beast frequently finds itself deluged with grant seekers and has built up defenses to fend them off. Therefore strategy and hard work is absolutely mandatory if one expects to make a conquest. When a relationship has been established, frequently the beast likes to become involved with the grant seeker and share in the process of developing a strategy. Be open to suggestions and procedures which will help you to receive a friendly response. The shy nature of the beast often means it will fail to respond to your inquiries. Therefore it is always wise to keep the initiative on your side.

The following pages explore in greater detail how one can prepare for this encounter. The grant seeker has an uphill struggle before him, but he can avoid many pitfalls by careful preparation and a general commitment to the task. By no means have we covered the whole subject, but hopefully you will find helpful clues and some insights into the rules of the "bread game."

2

Foundations:

Some Information You Need to Know

The following are some things it is useful to know about foundations before applying for a grant from them:

1) **Types of foundations.** Most foundations limit their field of activity in some way. Types of foundations include:

General Purpose Foundations. Most important of these are the particularly large foundations that operate with relatively few restrictions. They are the most difficult to obtain money from; generally they prefer to relate to institutions as large as they are.

Special Purpose Foundations. These restruct their grants to a specific area of interest: health, art, etc. They are a good source if your project falls within their area of interest.

Corporate or Company Foundations. Federal law allows a corporation to give 5% of its adjusted gross income to charitable and/or educational activities. Actually businesses now give on the average less than 2%, usually in uncreative grants to enhance their corporate image or to satisfy the personal preferences of investors or business contacts. Many corporations are getting edgy about flak they are receiving from the public for social irresponsibility, so they are now more susceptible to requests from ordinary folk. If a corporation has no foundation, try its public relations or community relations office.

Family Foundations. These are set up and controlled by a donor and his family; their grants fall within their areas of personal interest.

Community Foundations. A relatively recent addition to the foundation world, these foundations receive and grant funds within a specific geographic area. Often they are very large, since they receive the assets of smaller foundations who do not want to take the trouble to administer their funds themselves. Because they are limited in geographic area and have broad purposes, they are a good place to go for funds.

Wealthy Individuals. Many wealthy individuals do not have foundations of their own, but often make tax-deductible contributions to projects. There are all sorts of weird ways of finding these people: contribution reports of liberal political candidates, society pages of newspapers, friends and relatives, etc. They can be an excellent source of funds: first, because you don't have to go through a bureaucracy to contact them; second, because

14

they need the contact from non-wealthy people. Before you approach them, have everything together to make it easy for them to make a tax-deductible contribution to your group. Read carefully the legal and fiscal sponsor material in this book!

In addition to the above breakdown of areas of interests, past grantees are a very good source of information on a particular foundation. Every foundation must publish a list of its past grantees and keep it in its office.

2) Who makes the decisions. Most foundations have two levels of decision-making: a staff who screens proposals, interviews people, and does the legwork, and a board of trustees or directors who makes the final decisions, and usually talks only to the staff. Generally these latter people are white, middle- or upper-class men from business or professional backgrounds. Whatever you can find out in advance about their backgrounds, politics, interests, and so on will be useful in approaching them.

3) Time period between application and final decision on the proposal. Unless you have some heavy connections, this period is months, occasionally years, so plan ahead.

4) Average grant size. This is important. Don't submit a $100,000 program to a foundation that makes $10,000 grants, and, conversely, don't send a $2,500 request to the Ford Foundation.

Much of the above is public information. Foundations are required by law to keep a copy of their annual report, including grants lists, in their office and available to the public. Copies can also be obtained from the Internal Revenue Service office in Washington, D.C., at $1.00 per page. Most states have a registrar of charitable trusts office in the state capitol which keeps similar records. Also, a phone call or letter of inquiry to a foundation itself can get you some of the information. Don't forget past grantees as a useful source of information and experience.

Further information may be obtained from:

—**The Foundation Center**, at 888 Seventh Avenue, New York City, which collects and publishes all kinds of material on foundations. Local depositories for their publications and other current foundation information are: **Washington, D.C.**: The Foundation Center, Washington Office, 1001 Connecticut Avenue, N.W.; **San Francisco**: San Francisco Public Library, Business Branch, 530 Kearny Street; **Los Angeles**: University Research Library, Reference Department, University of California; **Atlanta**: Atlanta Public Library, 126 Carnegie Way, N.W.; **Chicago**: The Newberry Library, 60 W. Walton Street; **Boston**: Associated Foundation of Greater Boston, One Boston Place; **St. Louis**: The Danforth Foundation, 222 South Central Avenue; **Cleveland**: Cleveland Foundation Library, 700 National City Bank Building; **Austin**: Regional Foundation Library of the Hogg Foundation for Mental Health, University of Texas.

The following article was reprinted with permission from *Grantsmanship Center News* (October 1973, Vol. 1, No. 2)

THE $88.90 BASIC LIBRARY

There are many books and periodicals available related to funding and grantsmanship. Some are priced beyond the means of many non-profit agencies. Others may contain misinformation. We have prepared a list of basic books and periodicals that most agencies can afford, and that we feel most agencies should either own or have regular access to. We kept the total cost below $100. The fact that a publication is not on this list reflects no negative comment on its merit. This is only our economy-minded library package. In addition, having these publications, and knowing how to use them are two different things. In each issue of the "NEWS" we will highlight one or more of these publications, and give you some ideas on how they may be used. We welcome your comments and suggestions.

1. Catalog of Federal Domestic Assistance; sold on a subscription basis by the Superintendent of Documents, U.S. Government Printing Office, Washington, D.C. 20402—consists of a basic looseleaf manual describing in detail federal domestic assistance programs, with changes sent to you over a one-year period. The cost is $7.00 plus $2.50 for a binder which we recommend that you purchase also. **$9.50**

2. United States Government Organization Manual, 1973/74, is the official handbook of the Federal Government, containing descriptions of the legislative, judicial and executive branches, and of certain boards, commissions and committees. It is offered for sale by the Superintendent of Documents, U.S. Government Printing Office, Washington, D.C. 20402. The price is $3.00. **$3.00**

3. The Foundation Directory, Edition 4 (1971) costs $15.00, is published by The Foundation Center, but is purchased from Columbia University Press, 136 South Broadway, Irvington-on-Hudson, New York 10533. The Foundation Directory lists 5,454 grant-making foundations which had assets of $500,000 or more or which made grants of $25,000 or more in the year of record for the compilation of the Directory (1968, 1969, or early 1970 for this edition). Data on foundations, arranged by state, includes address, donor, purpose, financial information and names of officers and trustees. **$15.00**

4. The Foundation Center Information Quarterly, allows for updating of information in The Foundation Directory. It only lists changes from recent Directory data, obtained directly from the foundations or from their IRS returns, and relates to most foundations with assets of $1,000,000 or more. The Information Quarterly contains other information as well and is also available from the Columbia University Press at a cost of $7.50 per year. **$7.50**

5. The Foundation News, published bimonthly by The Council on Foundations, includes a variety of useful articles on foundations, and in addition contains the "foundation grants index," a section with removable pages reporting on foundation grants recently made in excess of $5,000. It costs $10 a year, and is available from Box 783, Old Chelsea Station, New York, N.Y. 10011. **$10.00**

6. The Foundation Grants Index, 1972, is a bound compilation of all grants which were reported in The Foundation News during 1972. It lists approximately 9,000 grants in excess of $10,000. The cost is $10.00 and it is available from the Columbia University Press, address above. **$10.00**

7. Developing Skills in Proposal Writing is written by Mary Hall, and is available for $10.00 from Continuing Education Publications, Waldo 100, Corvallis, Oregon 97331. This is the best, economically priced, proposal writing manual that we have seen. **$10.00**

8. Preparing Instructional Objectives, Robert F. Mager, Pearon Publications, San Francisco (1962). This publication will prove very useful as you seek to clarify the goals and objectives of your agency and of new programs that you are planning. It is a paperback and is nominally priced at $2.95. **$2.95**

9. The Bread Game: The Realities of Foundation Fundraising (Revised Edition) is available from Glide Publications, 330 Ellis Street, San Francisco, Ca. 94102. An inexpensive, valuable paperback. **$2.95**

10. Fund Raising Management is a bimonthly magazine published by Hoke Communications, 224 Seventh St., Garden City, Long Island, New York 11530. The cost is $8.00 a year. Though a commercial publication, laden with advertising for ashtrays emblazoned with your agency's crest, ads by fundraising firms, etc., this periodical will bring you an awareness of the non-grant areas of fundraising. It is especially helpful to those wishing to expand from a grants-only funding base, and seeking to learn more about how more traditional agencies mount their fundraising drives. **$8.00**

11. The Grantsmanship Center News, published ten times a year by The Grantsmanship Center, 7815 South Vermont Avenue, Los Angeles, California 90044. Subscription cost is $10.00 per year. We would be remiss if we did not recommend that you subscribe to our very own "NEWS," which we hope will become the very best, broad, inexpensive publication in the grantsmanship field. **$10.00**

TOTAL BASIC LIBRARY COST **$88.90**

3

Third World

Community:

A New Look

"Self-determination," "self-direction," "minority empowerment" are words synonymous with the word *survival* to Third World people. No longer are they content to have social, city, state, or federal agencies make unilateral decisions that affect their lives. They are now saying, "We will determine the need"; "We will chart the direction"; "We want to find our own solutions, our own alternatives, and we need money to do it." Thus, the grantsmanship game takes in new players.

These new players, the Third World community, will find they have a lot to learn: where the field is located, who's on the other team, what the rules are and what it takes to enter the competition. This chapter will give some tips on how to play the game.

To begin with, there are thousands of public, private and church foundations in the U.S. Obviously some systematic approach is needed, and a good place to begin is with your own geographical area. There are several advantages to approaching the community foundations first: a) generally, they gather information on the type of funding they can provide and annual reports are readily available, b) they usually meet at least once a month so there is no long waiting period, c) they usually maintain several full-time staff members who can help you locate other sources of funds, since they try to maintain close working relationships with private and family foundations.

Most major church denominations have established distribution funds to respond to Third World concerns. Some of these have been the first to understand and respond to the demand for self-determination and social change. They are an excellent source for seed money, technical assistance and endorsement for a project. A good portion of these funds is administered by Third World people.

New field players are the corporations and companies. Some of these players are in the game only to enhance their corporate image; however, some have taken the words "corporate responsibility" seriously and are trying to be open to new ways of funding and new approaches to old social problems. Colleges and universities, research, and scholarship funds seem to receive the largest share, but there are indications that some corporations are willing to fund projects dealing with prison and penal reform, economic development, etc. It's now an open field.

From a Third World perspective, wealthy individuals may be the most difficult source to reach. First, the opportunity to meet these people is limited, if not non-existent. Second, they don't want to be "hassled" for funds.

As much as your energy and patience will allow, try all these sources. Don't be misled by labels like "liberal" or "conservative" which others have attached to funding sources. What was liberal or progressive today may be conservative or reactionary tomorrow, and vice versa.

With rare exception, the other players in the game are white, middle-aged Protestant males in the upper social and economic levels of society (usually bankers, social scientists, businessmen, donors and peers of the donors, et al.). They comprise the boards of trustees, the staff, and the executive directors. Their interests, concerns, and understanding generally mirror their social and economic background. While board members usually make the final decisions, these decisions are based on the recommendations of the staff or executive directors. Since it is unusual for a board to go against the recommendation of its staff, it is the staff which you will have to reach.

If your project is located in a barrio or ghetto, there is little likelihood that you will be paid an on-site visit, so your proposal or presentation to them will have to suffice. Therefore, it is important to get the endorsement and support of people and groups working in similar areas. Credibility is important; they will check out who you know and work with and what your relationship is to similar organizations in your community.

Proposal-writing can be very frustrating, but it is a necessary evil. Don't rely on professional proposal writers; usually they are experts at cliches and literary rambling. You can do it yourself—you know and live with the problems. Don't get hung up in a long narrative of the history of oppression; try to get your point across in no more than six or eight pages. (The same advice goes for the interview as well.)

There is no easy way of liberating the bread but if you have your thing together, it can be done. You may then be on your way to taking self-determination and self-direction out of the theory phase into reality.

4

The Proposal:

How to Get It All Together

A proposal is only part of the grant process. Very few foundations fund programs by mail; a written request should be interesting enough to get people to meet with you. It should state your intentions and needs as clearly, simply, and briefly as possible. Limit it as much as possible to facts. Most proposals are too long, so when in doubt, cut things out. The essential elements are:

Cover Letter. Tell who you are and what you want to do; how much you need, when, and for how long; and where you are working now. Request a meeting: where you are is better, but more likely it will be at the foundation offices. It is very important that the information show how your project relates to the purposes of the foundation. If you are dealing with staff, or middle people, a good cover letter may be enough; you may not even need to submit a proposal until after you have met.

The cover letter is probably the first part of your proposal that any foundation person will see; therefore it is, in some ways, the most important part. If the person is turned on by the idea, he or she will probably read the rest of what you have written; if not, your whole proposal may be simply set aside. Test your letter on others before submitting it to anyone, and be prepared to rewrite again and again if necessary to come up with a statement that is short, clear, accurate, and interesting.

Overview. Describe the situation which your program is attempting to work on—drug crises, senior citizens and loneliness, medical services, etc.—and explain how and why you began the project. Mention here any money or materials which have been donated to you already, as evidence of community support. Be brief and to the point—one or two paragraphs should be enough.

Goals. Tell what you expect to accomplish, both long-range and within the period for which you have requested a grant. Avoid broad, sweeping generalizations and promising the impossible; one paragraph will do.

Implementation. Basically, tell exactly what you will be or are doing from day to day: who will be paid to do what, what facilities and equipment you will need, what services you will provide. This information should relate explicitly to the goals.

Structure. Describe what kind of structure you are building: broad-based community organization, small collective, etc. What is the control and decision-making process?

People. State who you are and what you have done in the past to demonstrate that you will do good work on the project in question. Remember that unless you have really good credibility with foundation people, it is a tactical error to hustle for a program that someone else will have to implement.

Budget. Detail your income and expenses. Note all sources of income: individual contributions, benefits, literature, sales, etc. Expenses include salaries to be paid, rent, phone, utilities, equipment, travel, and printing. Prepare carefully; make sure your figures add up. Don't bother to pad it; you'll have enough trouble getting what you need to get by on. If the project has been together for a while, prepare a financial statement showing your past expenditures. Preparing that is a valuable process for you, and it impresses foundation folks.

Future. Suggest what you are going to do when the grant runs out.

Addenda. These are your references. They can, and should, include people you serve or work with, and people who have credibility with the foundation. Professionals and past grantees of the foundation make good references. You will have to do some homework to find out who these people are and solicit their support. To-whom-it-may-concern letters aren't worth a damn. References should be ready to stick their necks out for you when questioned by foundation staff. Give the foundation their names and phone numbers.

Show your proposal to other people, especially your references, paying special attention to the suggestions of people who have dealt with the foundation before. If you meet with foundation people before you submit a proposal, ask for their help and suggestions in writing one.

Both the proposal and the covering letter should be typewritten and addressed specifically to the Executive Director, unless the foundation tells you to address it to someone else. Do not wait for the foundation to call you: wait a week or two after you send the letter or proposal and then call to set a time to meet with them.

You may submit the same proposal to several foundations, but frequently it is wise to tailor it to a particular foundation's interests. In any case, the covering letter should *always* be addressed to the particular foundation.

You may want to fit proposals to different institutions into an overall strategy. For example, one of the best ways to get a grant, especially from the larger foundations, is to have one already. There are two ways for new projects to take advantage of this. First, you can try to raise small "seed" contributions from local sources: churches, friends, or small foundations. This will get you known in your community, and will reassure larger foundations. Second is the great matching game. If you need $5,000, propose that a foundation put up half if you can come up with the rest. Then go to a second fund source and tell them you can match their grant. Foundations always like to see their money have more impact than its actual value. If you are matching money, work from small foundations to large, or between those of equal size. Don't go to a small local foundation to match a grant from the Ford Foundation. Also, don't try matching between fund sources who don't have compatible goals.

26

Securing funds from foundations is a slow and arduous process. Many months may elapse before you receive your first check. Be resourceful in keeping it together while you wait!

5

Sponsors:

Alternatives While
You Are Getting Incorporated

Federal law requires that foundations make grants to organizations for activities that are charitable, educational, or religious. There are some refinements, but, in theory, those are the only restrictions.

In practice, the situation is more complex. The Internal Revenue Service issues Letters of Exemption to groups which are incorporated for charitable, educational, or religious purposes. You have to submit applications for these letters, and you cannot even apply for one unless you are already a *non-profit corporation*. The time period between application and receipt of the letters varies from several weeks to two years.

The Internal Revenue Service Exemption Letters are supposed to accomplish several things. First, they provide good insurance (i.e., governmental approval) to donors that their donations are in fact tax-deductible. Second, they assure foundations that their incomes are exempt from federal tax. Finally, they give the federal government, particularly the IRS, a

29

means of controlling foundations and preventing tax rip-offs.

Keep in mind that nowhere does the law state that a foundation must make grants only to groups with IRS Exemption Letters; it is merely easier and safer to do so. The 1969 Federal Tax Reform Act provides that if any grant funds are misspent (the most glaring examples are influencing a public election or legislative act and supporting illegal actions, including civil disobedience), the granting foundation, its officers and staff are responsible. The government can impose penalties that include fines on the foundation and its staff; in extreme cases, it can even revoke the foundation's own tax-exempt status. Don't go overboard with sympathy, but understand that this situation has made foundation staff people and boards very uptight about to whom and how they give their money away, so that now virtually all granting foundations make grants *only* to groups with IRS Letters of Exemption. That gives the IRS a great deal of power in deciding who gets foundation money (you can guess how that works); and it makes it very difficult for any new group to get foundation money on its own, because of the long waiting period for the letters.

Here are some solutions to the problem. If your group is going to be around for a while, it is probably wise to incorporate and apply for IRS exemption. The legal section of this pamphlet is, we think, a good explanation of what that involves. Don't try to form a non-profit corporation by yourself. Get a lawyer, preferably one who is familiar with that area of the law. The process of incorporation itself is not that expensive: in California, for example, the filing fees are less than $50. However, the average attorney's fees for drawing up and filing incorporation papers are about $500. Rather than spend that much, seek out your nearest OEO-funded legal assistance project;

they should do it for free. If you can't do that, try recruiting a sympathetic local attorney.

If you want to apply for a grant before you have an IRS Exemption Letter, try to get an organization that does have such a letter to sponsor your project before you submit a proposal to a foundation. This is tricky, so first, a little background:

The IRS recognizes two kinds of exempt organizations (foundations): public and private. Public foundations, or public charities, include the major religious denominations and their member churches, organizations that receive substantial support (money) from the general public, and/or organizations that provide charitable and educational services to the public at large. They have fewer restrictions and reporting requirements than private foundations, and so make much better sponsors than private foundations. A good rule of thumb is always to use a public foundation as a sponsor.

Before you ask a public foundation to sponsor your project, make sure it really does have an IRS Exemption Letter as a public charity. Churches do not get individual Exemption Letters, but if they are part of a major denomination (Methodist, Catholic, Jewish, etc.) they are considered public charities. When in doubt, call a local IRS agent and ask him.

When a public foundation acts as your sponsor for a grant proposal it means, in effect, that the sponsor asks for the grant. It accepts legal and fiscal responsibility for whatever the project does. The sponsoring group receives the funds for the project, insuring a safe tax-deductible grant from the donor. The sponsor, in turn, pays the expenses of the project. Obviously the relationship between a project and a sponsor must be based on trust, honesty, and cooperation. Since they receive the money directly, sponsors may be required to submit written reports and financial statements to the foundation on how project funds are spent. You should be prepared to assist them in reporting and keeping track of money. For this work, some sponsors take a small percentage of the grant as a fee for their trouble. If the percentage is more than 10% of the grant, you are being gouged, so look elsewhere for a sponsor. Churches frequently sponsor projects for free.

A word of caution. The IRS might frown on the sponsor arrangement if the only connection between you and the sponsor is money. To avoid this, *select a sponsor whose goals are parallel to yours,* and who is interested in your project. The sponsor should support the project enough that it can fairly be treated as its own program as well as that of your group.

One other solution is to persuade a foundation to give you the money directly, even though you lack the IRS Exemption Letter. With most foundations this is extremely difficult, since it would require them to stick their necks out too far. You will need to convince them that you are capable of providing good, carefully written reports, including financial reports, when the grant is finished, to demonstrate how you spent the money. Failure to provide such reports gets the foundation in trouble and probably screws things up for the next group that tries to get funded directly. Read the chapters on bookkeeping and reporting which follow in this book.

A final alternative to sponorship is to arrange a conditional loan from a prospective grantor. Suppose, for example, that you know someone who wants to give your group $1,000, wants a tax deduction, and for some reason or other does not want to give the money to your sponsor. What you can do is have that person *loan* you the $1,000 on the condition that the loan will be forgiven and transformed into a gift at the moment that your group gets its tax deduction.

You both win: you have immediate use of the money, and the donor either gets his money back or gets a tax deduction.

6

Formation of a
Tax-Exempt Organization:

A Drag But Necessary

The purpose of this section is to describe the procedures followed by most organizations which want to obtain tax-exempt status and to allow donors tax deductions for contributions.*

1. **Purposes.** The first step, prior to the actual formation of the organization, is to determine whether the purposes and activities of the proposed organization satisfy the requirements for tax exemption. To qualify as tax-exempt so that donors can obtain tax deductions for their contributions, the organization must qualify under section 501(c)(3) of the Internal Revenue Code of 1954. That section exempts:

> . . . Corporations, and any community chest, fund or foundation organized and operated exclusively for religious, charitable, scientific, testing for public safety, literary, or educational pur-

---

* If your organization resides outside of the State of California you should check with a local attorney and/or the Secretary of State regarding local incorporation procedures and requirements.

poses, or for the prevention of cruelty to animals, **no part of the net earnings of which inures to the benefit of any private shareholder or individual, no substantial part of the activities of which is carrying on propaganda, or otherwise attempting to influence legislation, and which does not participate in (including the publishing or distributing of statements), any political campaign on behalf of any candidate for public office.**

The language in that section has been interpreted by numerous court decisions and Internal Revenue Service regulations and rulings. Your lawyer or accountant must determine whether your organization's proposed purposes and activities satisfy those interpretations.

2. **Formations.** The next step is to form your organization. Most tax-exempt organizations are formed as non-profit corporations. This entails: (1) selecting a name for the organization that is not held or used by any other corporation in your state; (2) drafting Articles of Incorporation, bylaws, and, if necessary (see below) an application for exemption from state income tax; (3) holding the first meeting of the board where ordinarily bylaws are adopted, officers are elected, a corporate seal is adopted, and an officer is authorized to do all acts necessary to obtain state and federal tax exemptions.

3. **State Filing.** If your state has an income tax, you may have to apply for a separate state tax exemption. In California, you file your application for state exemption (Form FTB 3500) with the California Franchise Tax

Board, and the Articles of Incorporation with the Secretary of State. Once the Franchise Tax Board grants the California tax exemption, the Secretary of State will file the Article of Incorporation. At this point, your organization is, officially, a non-profit corporation exempt from California franchise tax, and you should file copies of the Articles of Incorporation with the Clerk of the county in which your organization works.

4. **Federal Filing.** The application for a federal tax exemption (Form 1023) should now be completed and filed on behalf of the organization. If the application is successful, you will receive a determination letter from the District Director of the Internal Revenue Service, granting your exemption and explaining your responsibilities under the law. Particular attention should be paid to the private formation/public charity questions on the form.

The amount of time these steps will take depends, in large part, on how knowledgeable and efficient you and your lawyer or accountant are. The first step is often the most time-consuming, because formulating your purposes and activities requires a lot of detailed thought about the precise nature of your organization. The timing for the second step depends almost entirely upon your lawyer or accountant; one month seems to be common. The third step, filings at the state and local levels, can usually be accomplished in California in a month or so, depending on the backlog of applications in the Franchise Tax Board. But the fourth and critical step, obtaining a federal tax exemption, can take incredibly long. If the organization's purposes and activities are straightforward and typical (in the eyes of the IRS), and if the local office of the IRS is not required to refer the application to Washington under its internal rules, a favorable IRS determination letter can be obtained in several weeks. More commonly, however, it takes about three months to obtain an exemption.

The cost of forming a tax-exempt organization can vary greatly depending on the fees charged by its lawyer or accountant. A few organizations exist which might provide free legal assistance to tax-exempt organizations, if their purposes are deemed worthwhile, but we are unaware of similar organizations that provide free accounting services. Apart from these fees, however, in California, the other costs of formation—corporate seal and filing fees to the Secretary of State and County Clerk—should be less than $50.00.

Reporting to the Government: Private Foundation or Public Charity? You will be required to report to various government agencies when your organization has been formed and is operating. Many of the reporting requirements differ, depending upon whether your organization qualifies under federal law as a favored "public charity" or a disfavored "private foundation." All Section 501(c)(3) organizatios s are classified as either public charities or private foundations, depending on their sources of financial support. Most of the public charity categories require that your organization obtain a certain percentage of its income from "the public"—i.e., small contributors or grants from the government or other public charities.

If your organization is a "private foundation" in the eyes of the IRS, it must meet the following reporting requirements to the Internal Revenue Service *withis 4½ months after the close of its tax year:*

1. Form 990-PF
2. Form 990-AR (an annual report)
3. A copy of a newspaper ad advising the public that it may inspect your annual report at your office within six months.

Each state will have additional reporting requirements of its own. In California, these are:

1. *To the California Franchise Tax Board:* Form
199, due with a $5.00 fee within 4½ months after the
close of the organization's tax year.

2. To the Registry of Charitable Trusts:
— Registration Form, due within 6 months from
the date that the organization authorizes its first
distribution. (This is a one-time requirement.)
— A copy of your IRS Form 199, due within 4½
months after the end of the organization's tax
year.

3. *To the state attorney general:* A copy of Form
990-AR, due on the same date as above.

As a private foundation, your organization will also
have extensive reporting requirements to all private
foundation grantors.

Finally, if your organization is an existing private
foundation, you may want to consult your lawyer to
make certain that it has complied with the new tax
law requiring certain amendments to the organization's Articles of Incorporation.

As you can see, the legal side of forming and operating a tax-exempt organization takes time and effort.
It will test your dedication and seriousness of purpose, but it will also impress the hell out of contributors, grant-making foundations and, probably,
yourself.

INVOICE PAST DUE

PAYMENT

FINAL TYPING

RECEIVED

Return Receipt Req

COPY

PAID

X

STATE WH/TAX

RECEIVED

X

OK FOR FINAL TYPING

STATUTE OF LIMITATION

MEMO

REFUND

RECEIVED

OF STOCK

PAYMENT

DOCUMENTARY TRANSFER TAX $........

COMPUTED ON FULL VALUE

COMPUTED ON FULL VALUE

REMAINING THEREON

STATE WH/TAX

Only 5% use Tax applicable.

REFUND

COPY

SIGNATURE OF DECLARANT OR AGENT

RECEIVED

NOT RETURNABLE

X

PAID

ORIGINAL INVOICE

STATUTE OF LIMITATION

PAID

MEM

TRANSFER TAX $

PUTED ON FULL VALUE OF PROPERTY CONVEYED, OR

UTED ON FULL VALUE LIENS & ENCUMBRANCES

ING ON AT TIME OF SALE.

MAILED

INVOICE PAST DUE

X

PAID

ARANT OR AGENT DETERMIN

RM NAME

FINANCE CHARGE

NEW BALANCE

BILLED

PAID

COPY

STATE WH/TAX

LLED

URNABLE

BILLED

BILL

7

Suggested Accounting Procedures for Grantees:

Do It Right the First Time

The importance of good accounting procedures for all organizations cannot be overstated. Too many groups tend to feel that anyone can keep a set of books. Don't be sucked into this attitude—it can be your undoing. Keep good records from the beginning. Ask the help of a good accountant to at least get the books set up in good order. Even though you may write your own checks, make all your own deposits and do your own posting. Check back with your accountant every three months so that your books can be reviewed and checked over for accuracy. A good set of books will go a long way toward convincing foundations and other contributors that you are a responsible group.

This chapter is primarily designed for groups handling less than $10,000.00 a year. If you are fortunate enough to have more than this amount, go directly to your accountant: you need one.

Good records are necessary for:
- good internal management;
- federal and state tax requirements;
- reporting for foundations, both present and prospective.

Good record keeping does not have to be burdensome. It just has to be accurate and complete. A simplified worksheet such as that following page 48 in this book is all that is needed for a small project. A larger project should consult with a CPA knowledgeable in the field of non-profit organizations in order to set up a comprehensive set of accounting records which will satisfy foundation and governmental authorities as well as its own board of directors.

It is important that funds of non-profit organizations be kept segregated. The reason for this is that foundations like to know how their funds were disbursed. If you get several grants, it's very difficult to tell which money went for what purpose. *Open separate checking accounts for each grant* and keep a separate worksheet on each.

There are several areas of record keeping which may create problems:

Cash. Open a checking account as soon as you receive a grant award. Get a commercial-type checkbook which allows you to record the following on the check stub:
1) Date
2) Payee
3) Amount
4) Description

The check stub is the initial source of your record-keeping information. Make sure it is completely filled out. Try not to make checks out to "cash"; it is often difficult to determine what the disbursement was for.

Prepare a bank reconciliation every month, following the instructions on the back of your bank statement. A bank reconciliation allows you to determine that all deposits have been properly made and that your bank balance and checkbook balance are correct. Make sure that a running balance is kept in the checkbook so that you know how much cash you have on hand.

If it is necessary to keep petty cash, use the following method. Set a limit of $25.00 to $50.00 on your petty cash fund. Draw the initial check for the fund. As money is taken out of the fund for postage, travel, etc., submit a voucher and receipts containing:

1) Date
2) Payee
3) Amount
4) Type of expense

When the fund is depleted, summarize the expenditures and draw a check for the difference. The change in the fund plus vouchers should always equal the limit ($25.00 to $50.00) set up.

It is advisable that bill-paying authority and check-writing authority be solely in the hands of the director of the project. He also should be responsible for depositing cash received by the organization.

Files. A good filing system is also important. This can be very easily put together. The file should be divided as follows:

1) Permanent
2) Correspondence
3) Program
4) Accounting
   a) Bank statements and canceled checks
   b) Cash receipts
   c) Accounts payable/paid bills

The permanent file should have separate folders for legal papers, tax records, grant documents, etc.

The correspondence file should be the receptacle for all correspondence into and out of the organization. Letters should be filed on an A-Z basis in chronological order.

The program file can be arranged at the discretion of the organization. It will include work papers, memos, written reports, etc., relating to project activity.

Paid and unpaid bills should be properly filed. All unpaid bills should be kept in one folder marked "unpaid bills"; these should be reviewed at least twice a month (the 1st and 15th) and paid. For the paid bills, set up an A-Z file. As a bill is paid, mark it "paid." Write the check number, payment date and amount on ths bill. This voids the bill and prevents double payment.

One file for cash receipts memoranda, duplicate deposit slips, etc., should suffice. Bank statements and canceled checks should be filed together with a separate file folder for each month.

Payroll Taxes. We will not go into the problems of payroll taxes, but if you have employees, contact your local federal and state authorities: the Internal Revenue Service and (in California) the Department of Human Resources Development. Call them up— they will be listed in your phone book—and make an appointment to see them in person. Tell them your situation. They will give you the forms and information that you will need in order to comply with federal and state laws.

Worksheet. The worksheet is designed to allow you to keep track of grant expenditures in a way that will not be burdensome to you, but at the same time will allow you to have at your fingertips the information you need to prepare financial statements, foundation reports, and federal and state income tax returns.

The worksheet is very simple to use and does not require a clerical background. Use a separate sheet for each grant so that each grant can be separately accounted for. Worksheets can be obtained at any stationery store; ask for 14-column accountants' workpaper (or larger if you wish). Head up the columns as in the example which follows. The expense categories are based upon the budget categories in the grant. The information for the worksheet will come from the stubs in the checkbook.

Cash receipts. In the example $8,000.00 was received from the Eldridge Foundation on January 1. It is the first entry in January. There is no need to label it if all receipts into the account will be grant revenue from the same foundation.

Cash disbursements. Typical monthly disbursements for the months of January and February are shown. Each disbursement should be categorized. The total of the categories will equal the total cash disbursed.

Balance. This is self-explanatory.

Totals and sub-totals. As shown at the end of June and December, expenses over a period of several months can be accumulated. This will give you the figures you need to fill out financial statements, tax returns, and foundation reports. You may need the advice of an accountant at this point to set up the appropriate financial statement format or fill out some of the year-end tax returns.

Payroll. Each employee is required to have an employee earnings card. An example of an earnings card for Jo Ann Grok is included. Her salary for January is as follows:

Gross Wages		250.00
FICA	$13.00	
W/H	34.50	
SDI	2.50	
	50.00	50.00
Net		200.00

See the worksheet in January for the method of recording the salary. For simplicity, the total withholding of $50.00 is recorded as a credit. Withholding details are recorded on the payroll card. When tax payment is made (worksheet February 7), total payment ($126) is divided in two: (1) the employee's share ($95.00) is charged to Payroll Taxes Payable in column 8 and withheld from the employee's paycheck, and (2) employer's share ($31.00) is charged to fringe benefits for Taxes and Licenses in columns 13 and 14. (See note 2 on page 2 of worksheet.)

Employee vs. Independent Contractor. Ordinarily, payroll taxes are applicable only if an *employer-employee* relationship exists. Because of serious penalties for failure to properly withhold payroll taxes, be aware of an employer-employee relationship when it exists. Determining whether a party performing a service is an employee includes: (1) the *right* to control the worker (even if the right is not exercised), (2) duration of the job, (3) method of payment (hourly or by the job), (4) exclusive right to services, (5) does he make an investment in facilities and equipment (indicating an independence), and (6) is there an opportunity for profit and loss (indicating an independence).

If you are dealing with an independent contractor (i.e. consultant, attorney or CPA), you should contract for such services in writing. All payments to independent contractors should *only* be made upon presentation of a written statement, so that you have a record of payment. How to record salaries and payroll withholding is explained on page 44.

This brief chapter should help you set up an adequate system of record keeping for your project. If the suggestions here are properly followed, your project work will be easier and many problems that might arise in the future will be prevented.

46

Sample Bookkeeping Documents

RECORD OF EMPLOYMENT AND EARNINGS

NAME Jo Ann Grok	**S.S. NO.** 554-46-4592
ADDRESS 7 Clayton St.	**WORK** Organizer
CITY San Francisco	**DEPT.** - -
SINGLE OR MARRIED M	**SALARY**
NUMBER OF DEPENDENTS 2	**DATE STARTED** 1/1/70
WITHHOLDING STATUS M-2	**DATE LEFT**
REMARKS	**REASON**

19

	TOT. EARNINGS	EMP. INS.	O.A.B.	WITHHOLDING TAX
FIRST QUARTER	750 00	7 50	39 00	103 50
SECOND QUARTER	750 00	7 50	39 00	103 50
THIRD QUARTER	750 00	7 50	39 00	103 50
FOURTH QUARTER	750 00	7 50	39 00	103 50
TOTAL AMOUNT	3000 00	30 00	156 00	414 00

FIRST QUARTER

WEEK ENDING Month	TOTAL WAGES	STATE U. INS.	FED. O.A.B.	WITH'G TAX		TOTAL	NET PAYMENT
Jan	250 00	2 50	13 00	34 50			200 00
Feb	250 00	2 50	13 00	34 50			200 00
March	250 00	2 50	13 00	34 50			200 00
TOTAL	750 00	7 50	39 00	103 50			600 00

THIRD QUARTER

WEEK ENDING	TOTAL WAGES	STATE U. INS.	FED. O.A.B.	WITH'G TAX		TOTAL	NET PAYMENT
July	250 00	2 50	13 00	34 50			200 00
Aug.	250 00	2 50	13 00	34 50			200 00
Sept.	250 00	2 50	13 00	34 50			200 00
TOTAL	750 00	7 50	39 00	103 50			600 00

SECOND QUARTER

	TOTAL WAGES	STATE U. INS.	FED. O.A.B.	WITH'G TAX		TOTAL	NET PAYMENT
April	250 00	2 50	13 00	34 50			200 00
May	250 00	2 50	13 00	34 50			200 00
June	250 00	2 50	13 00	34 50			200 00
TOTAL	750 00	7 50	39 00	103 50			600 00
TOTAL 6 MOS.	1500 00	15 00	78 00	207 00			1200 00

FOURTH QUARTER

	TOTAL WAGES	STATE U. INS.	FED. O.A.B.	WITH'G TAX		TOTAL	NET PAYMENT
Oct.	250 00	2 50	13 00	34 50			200 00
Nov.	250 00	2 50	13 00	34 50			200 00
Dec.	250 00	2 50	13 00	34 50			200 00
TOTAL	750 00	7 50	39 00	103 50			600 00
TOTAL 12 MOS.	3000 00	30 00	156 00	414 00			2400 00

The UTILITY Line Form No. 65-021 (21 Pad) — 38-021 (21) — Loose Leaf — 55-021 (21) Bank

8

Reporting on a Grant:

The Paper Work

After you receive a foundation grant, you will be asked to submit a report to the foundation accounting for the use of the grant funds as soon as they are spent. This is important because the Internal Revenue Service requires that foundations have such reports from all their grantees. Don't make a lot of work for yourself; all you have to do is assure foundation people (who are a little paranoid by nature) that you did spend their money the way you said you would.

The following is a hypothetical project description and report we prepared that should be adequate. There are two parts: a written description and a listing of project expenditures. The hypothetical situation is as follows:

On January 1, 1971, the (Name) Foundation made a grant to the San Francisco Tenants' Union. The grant was in the amount of $10,000 for the period of one year, for the purpose of operating an office and paying the salaries of the organizers of the project to enable them to educate tenants about their legal and civil rights in housing and to help indigent tenants bring about improvements in housing for low-income people.

A copy of the Grant Agreement follows:

49

HYPOTHETICAL GRANT AGREEMENT

On _____ *January 1, 1971* _____ , The (Name) Foundation (Grantor) granted to _____ *S.F. Tenants'* *Union* _____ (Grantee) the amount of *$10,000.00*, payable _____ *1/1/71* _____ , for purposes stated in the cover letter accompanying this Agreement. Grantee agrees and consents to the following conditions of the grant:

1. Grantee shall use the grant solely for the purposes stated in the accompanying cover letter, and Grantee shall repay to Grantor any portion of the amount granted which is not used for the purposes of the grant.

2. Grantee shall submit a report to Grantor when it has spent all the granted funds or one year from this date, whichever occurs first. Such report shall describe the progress that Grantee has made toward achieving the purposes for which this grant was made and shall detail all expenditures made from the granted funds. If Grantee expends the granted funds over a period longer than one year from this date, Grantee shall submit such reports, as described above, annually upon the anniversary date of this grant until the funds have been exhausted, at which time Grantee shall submit a final report.

3. Grantee shall show these grant funds separately on its books. All expenditures made in furtherance of the purposes of the grant shall be charged off against the grant and shall appear on those books. Grantee shall keep records to substantiate such expenditures. Grantee shall make such books and records available to the Grantor at reasonable times. Grantee shall keep copies of all books and records and all reports to Grantor for at least four years after completion of the use of the grant funds.

4. Grantee shall not use any portion of the funds granted herein to carry on propaganda or otherwise to attempt to influence specific legislation, either by direct or grassroots lobbying, nor to influence the outcome of any specific public election, nor to carry on directly or indirectly a voter registration drive, nor to make grants to individuals on a non-objective basis, nor to use the funds for any non-charitable or non-educational purposes.

5. If this grant is made for the purpose of capital equipment or for endowment, Grantee shall submit reports to Grantor for this taxable year and for Grantee's two succeeding taxable years describing the use of the principal and income (if any) derived from the granted funds.

IN WITNESS WHEREOF, this Grant Agreement is signed this _____ day of _____ , _____.

San Francisco Tenants' Union
(Grantee)

By _____
(director of Grantee)

HYPOTHETICAL GRANTEE REPORT

The San Francisco Tenants' Union opened an office at 1358 McAllister Street in the Western Addition district of the city on February 3, 1971.

Most of the residents of the Western Addition area are black people with low incomes derived from menial jobs or welfare assistance. Because of low income and racial discrimination in other neighborhoods, many Western Addition residents have been compelled to rent apartments in dilapidated and unsafe buildings, with no option of moving to apartments in better condition. When individual tenants made complaints to their landlords or city health and building authorities about housing conditions, they were either ignored or evicted in violation of their legal rights.

The two organizers paid by the grant from The (Name) Foundation enlisted the help of the Neighborhood Legal Assistance office in preparing a handbook of the legal rights of tenants, and in handling individual tenants' legal cases on a referral basis from our office. With this support, we were able to provide individual counseling to an average of ten low-income tenants a day. Tenants' problems included: eviction due to non-payment of rent, threats of eviction without legal grounds, repairs required under health, fire and safety codes, and violations of leases or rent agreements. In some cases, such as evictions without legal grounds, the tenant was able to solve his own problem once we had informed him of his legal rights. Other cases were solved by having an attorney, who volunteered to represent the tenant, call the landlord; this frequently was enough to induce the landlord to withdraw the threat of eviction or correct the problem.

The individual counseling occupied much of the full-time organizers' and six neighborhood volunteers' time. However, our main interest was to convince tenants that their problems could only be solved in the long run by organizing themselves. As a group they would be able to put significant pressure on landlords to provide decent housing at a reasonable rent. We began organizing among tenants of single multi-unit apartment buildings. This was particularly easy to do with tenants of very dilapidated buildings, a number of whom had already come to the office with individual complaints. Usually we prepared and distributed a leaflet to building residents pointing out the problems and setting a date, time and place for tenants to meet and discuss possible ways of solving the problems. We then met with the tenants and told them about their legal rights to take such actions as withholding rent money until legally required repairs were made, and assisting them in drawing up a list of their needs to negotiate with the landlord and to write into a mutually satisfactory and legally binding contract between tenants and landlord.

There were a number of significant obstacles to this kind of organizing. First, tenants usually waited until a crisis like a huge rent raise or physical malfunction before they sought any help. Before that time they had seen no need to organize, and once the crisis arose, it was more difficult to get the group to deal with it constructively. Secondly, tenants were reluctant to speak up about housing problems for fear of retaliatory eviction. The availability of volunteer attorneys helped this problem. Finally, because of poverty, unemployment and dilapidated housing, many tenants are transient. Ironically, one good way to stop the cycle of transience from one slum dwelling to another was organizing tenants, but a building whose tenants are changing every few months is difficult to organize.

We were successful in helping the tenants of three buildings form groups this year that negotiated rent and repair contracts with their landlords. In one building physical conditions were so bad, and the landlord so unconcerned, that is was necessary for the tenants to withhold their rent money, placing it in a trust fund until the landlord agreed to make necessary repairs and sign a contract with the tenants.

More recently, one of our organizers did a study of building ownership in the Western Addition. He identified several people with large slum property holdings in the neighborhood, and our most recent organizing effort has been among tenants of all the buildings owned by one of these "slumlords." We feel that this approach will have more leverage in improving housing conditions than counseling single tenants or organizing one building at a time.

The grant for the first year's expenses to the San Francisco Tenants' Union enabled us to do effective work improving housing conditions in the Western Addition, but there is still a lot left to do. This year we have sought and received enough small donations from neighborhood residents and churches to pay for office expenses and some supplies. The Neighborhood Legal Assistance office found funds to hire the two organizers paid formerly by grant funds to continue working with the Tenants' Union, and there are now about ten volunteers working with us regularly.

HYPOTHETICAL REPORT
OF GRANT EXPENDITURE

Grant No. 337 from The (Name) Foundation to:

San Francisco Tenants' Union
200 Bush Street
San Francisco, California

Project period:

From January 1, 1972 to December 31, 1972

Reporting period:

From January 1, 1972 to December 31, 1972

Expenditures:
Personnel:

Salary	6,000	
Fringe Benefits	356	
	6,356	6,356
Rent		1,200
Telephone & Answering Service		840
Utilities		200
Supplies		344
Travel		190
Secretarial Service		980
TOTAL		**10,110**

9

Two Sample

Proposals:

How Somebody Else Did It

When confronted with the task of writing a proposal, be it for $1,000 or $100,000, most who have never embarked on this treacherous trail before express the wish that they could look at somebody else's efforts in this area. It must be said that there is no single model or way of approaching the task. Proposals as short as two pages or as long as twenty-five pages have all been funded somewhere along the way.

With fear and trepidation two proposals have been included in *The Bread Game*. While they are well written, don't be overwhelmed by them. Be yourself and express in your own words what it is that you are all about. Don't overstate or understate — don't promise what you can't produce, or neglect those areas of your project which will be of interest to the foundation.

Look over the following pages and realize that all things are possible.

JAPANESE COMMUNITY YOUTH COUNCIL:
FUNDING PROPOSAL

SUMMARY OF PROPOSAL

Youth has historically been among the most disenfranchized segments of this society. In America, to be young *and* of the colored ethnic groups is double oppression. The Japanese Community Youth Council of San Francisco has, for the past three years, been trying to effect a change at these two levels. The focus has been on Japanese American youth – *sansei*, as they are called by members of the Japanese community. The overall goal is to organize youth to mobilize for change and to return strength and autonomy to a fragmented community.

Community development in order to attain community control involves a slow but consistent input of energy into programs that will meet current needs and thus build a base on which further change can be implemented. But if these programs are to be cohesive, a full-time coordinator must be present and working. This proposal requests funds to pay the salaries of a staff director and an administrative assistant for JCYC. The amount requested is $300 per month for each position for a period of six months. This totals $3,600. Funding for salaries is proposed because this area is the most difficult for which to obtain grants. Supplies and operating expenses are easy to come by from the established funding sources. Salaries for an overall programs director are not.

OVERVIEW

The Japanese community in San Francisco, as a whole, has very little political consciousness. The reasons for this stem from a history of manipulation by the American government and by the value systems held by the ruling class.

After the World War II concentration camp experience, Japanese in America were prone to believe that the reason for their confinement was their high visibility. They had clustered into *nihonmachi*s or Japanesetowns and had become highly successful and a potential economic threat to established power holders. In order to prevent this condition of high visibility from occurring again and to prove their loyalty to America, they became the "Quiet Americans." Assimilation in order to survive was the prime objective. As a result, Japanese Americans became labeled the "model minority," a concept to be used against Blacks, Chicanos, and other Third World people in their struggle for equal rights and ethnic identity.

In this process of assimilation, Japanese Americans, especially the youth, were losing their cultural identity. Sansei were confronted by the contradictions of being "almost white" and yet not having the status of whites. Questions of "Who am I?" and "What does it mean to be Japanese American?" were unanswered.

The contradictions came to a peak in 1968 during the Third World strikes at the University of California at Berkeley and San Francisco State College. The strikes demanded Third World studies and more EOP funding. When ethnic studies were finally implemented, Japanese American students realized that it was necessary for students to return to their respective communities and organize there. The reasons were twofold. Youth was seeking answers to the previously mentioned questions. But concommitant with this was the need to redefine the Japanese commun-

60

ity—the need to affect the "mainstream" mentality of Japanese Americans. Youth needed to build viable alternatives within the community to challenge the racist and capitalist institutions of which Third World people have no control: in other words, to develop a strong, autonomous, and politically conscious Japanese community.

GOALS AND PHILOSOPHY

The San Francisco Japanese Community Youth Council, Inc., was formed in early 1969. It was, at that time, a council of fourteen Japanese youth organizations, ranging from church groups, Boy Scouts, and Girl Scouts to the Asian American Political Alliance and the George Washington High School United Asian American Students.

JCYC was a step towards breaking down some of the negative values of American society—values such as nonproductive competition among the youth and regarding youth as a group which requires authoritative direction. The growing alienation in youth caused by their lack of power to change or control the forces which affect their lives could be alleviated with an organization which was an open forum to air problems and then to confront them.

Eventually, programs were implemented. These were twofold in their approach. One purpose was to have programs which would deal with unmet needs: draft help, counseling for youth on family, school, and legal problems, jobs (both referral and actual employment). The second purpose was to have programs organized and run by youth themselves. Activities which were enjoyed by youth were organized into a more structured format. Arts and crafts, ceramics, photography, and daycamp were such youth-run programs.

The following are the programs run during the spring of 1972:

Community Counseling Service. There are many areas of social needs in the community which are not being met. Some of the biggest problems are among young people. Among these are drug abuse, identity crisis, draft, and cultural alienation, manifesting in family problems. There are no existing community programs to deal with the problems facing many sansei and yonsei (fourth generation Japanese Americans) and their families. CCS was established to deal with some of these problems.

The objective of CCS is to create a program which provides a "culturally relevant" counseling service for the Japanese community. The objective will be met first by implementing intense internal education within the group of counselors. This is to maintain a consistency of approach with the various cases and to give CCS the stability it will need to breed stability within others. The work areas to be covered by CCS include drug abuse, counseling, draft counseling, family counseling, run-away and predelinquent cases, all for which there is training and evaluation. In addition to these services, CCS is organizing a parents' group in conjunction with the programs directed toward grammar-school-age children.

Job Referral. In the past, JCYC has received information on job offerings, but has had no means for filling those jobs. Conversely, there have been young people who were looking for jobs, but none were available. In order to alleviate this, it was felt that there should be a way in which young people could find information on jobs, and also a way in which to fill job openings. As a result, the idea of a job referral program was created to tie the two ends together.

The goal of the program is to provide a job referral agency where information on job openings can be obtained and where jobs can be filled from a job pool. The program is geared towards youth in need of part-time jobs. Arrangements are being made with agencies, businesses, HRD, etc., in which available jobs will be given to JCYC to fill, and in which special job programs (STEP, NYC) will be set aside specifically for JCYC. JCYC will then become the youth-servicing agency for the Japanese community with official recognition. The emphasis of the program should not be merely to get people jobs, but to have those who use the service to relate to JCYC as a whole, to its goals, and to the community in general. Also, jobs should be in the community, if at all possible, doing community-based work (as can be done with STEP and NYC).

Tutoring: The purpose of this program is to provide assistance to students who need help in courses which they do not understand. There are many students taking courses in junior high and senior high schools who have teachers who fail to consider the intake of information by the student and merely assume that the student should be at a certain level. This assumption fails to take into consideration the cultural background of the student. The student loses interest and fails to see any relevancy in the course. Many of these students cut class and roam around with their peers. The student falls behind and finds it difficult to catch up ... the student flunks the course.

Tutoring is designed to teach the student to survive in this society. He learns to discriminate between relevant subjects and those which do not pertain to him as an ethnic minority. He also learns to perceive subject matter as well as the "educational" process from an Asian American viewpoint. The student becomes aware of the contradictions in the educational system—that courses are taught based on a white upper-class standard; that minorities are placed in lower tracks ending in vocational training while the white students are in the upper tracks leading to college; that the tracking system is based on an IQ test created on white middle-class standards; that minorities are kept out of college education; and that the cycle begins all over again. Tutoring teaches the student to see this vicious cycle and to work to change it by breaking one of the links in the chain.

Children's Program. The Children's Program is important because it serves as an alternative to the educational system and similar programs offered by other groups. The values which are stressed are working cooperatively, rather than competitively, treating everyone equally and openly. Through the activities and field trips, friendships are formed between child and counselor which do not have a chance of being formed in other places.

The objectives are to develop leadership in the children, self-reliance and self-confidence; to stress cooperation and sharing; to offer knowledge in the areas of first aid, science, music, and drama, in a way which is both fun and exciting; to provide an opportunity for children to develop their creativity; to have fun learning and playing together. The objectives will be met through the activities which are planned, e.g., arts and crafts, field trip, games and songs. Most important are the relationships which the counselors establish with children. It is through these, on a one-to-one basis, that most of the learning will take place: not only knowledge of things, but also of people, and trying out new values in relation to them.

Emergency School Assistance Program (ESAP). JCYC and the Community Youth for Action, in a joint sponsorship, received a $53,744 grant from the Department of Health, Education and Welfare, to operate a project under the Emergency School Assistance Program's community group category.

The project is an educational, remedial and cultural development project. The goal of the project is "conflict resolution" for students affected directly by the Desegregation Plan. The project will accomplish this goal by focusing on four general areas: (1) social/cultural; (2) skill development/self-expression; (3) educational/remedial; (4) human relations/multi-racial education. The vehicle used to deal with these areas is instructional in nature. Classes will be held in two centers, operating in the community. They will be offered in combined Black and Asian history and culture, reading, sewing, arts and ceramics, and music and drama. Also offered are tutoring, counseling, and bilingual counseling and information. The classes will have qualified people recruited from the community in charge and will also utilize the energy, assistance, and expertise of parents, teachers, and other community people on a volunteer basis.

The project is open to all elementary students in zone one of the San Francisco Unified School District's Desegregation Plan. Our emphasis, however, is on helping Black and Asian students residing in the Western Addition. Students will be accepted in the program either by volunteer signup or referral. The referral may come from parents, teachers or social agencies. There is no cost or fee for students in the project. Parents must give their permission for their children to be enrolled in the program. Supervision will be given the students from the time they are released from school until they reach home after the classes.

The project will operate out of two centers, one located at 1732 Buchanan Street and the other at 1016 McAllister Street. The centers will be open from 1:00 p.m. to 7:00 p.m. Classes will be scheduled during this period. This is an after-school project. Special programs are planned, such as field trips and other kinds of outings for the purpose of cultural enrichment. The project is funded for one year and will run continuous with the school calendar. Enrollment will be open on a continuous basis.

It has been the continuing belief of JCYC that it sponsors programs which will serve the youth and are run by youth. In this aspect, JCYC is unique within San Francisco's Japanese community. It is the only youth organization (e.g., Scouts, churches, schools, etc.) that is not under adult/parent or institutional authority. But because of this philosophy, attaining credibility within the community has been a slow and lengthy process. The Japanese community is strongly age-oriented (children must obey their parents) and tradition plays a major role. This tradition stems from feudal Japan — the era during which Issei immigrated to America. And these traditions coincide with the American society's values.

Coping with this situation while promoting change means that first it is important for JCYC to provide programs which will gain the trust of the people. In this regard, the summer daycamp program was the best public relations tool for JCYC. The summer daycamp program enrolled ninety children. These children went home each day with enthusiastic reports of what they had done that day. This is the best type of PR for any youth organization. This gaining trust is the first step for any credible organizing group.

When speaking of community control in terms of sansei, one has to consider the circumstances within which one is working. Factors such as history, culture, language, peer group pressure, and forces outside the community will inevitably affect the tactics which are used to gain control. Understanding this, it is necessary that any community-based organization provide concrete programs which reflect and implement the philosophy of the organization, as opposed to presenting the ideology dogmatically to the community without producing constructive programs. The basis of work is directed outward for the community, not inward for one's own ego and ideology.

JCYC sees steps towards gaining community control. Community control means an accumulation of several points. Some of these are having the power to determine the economics of the community (i.e., redevelopment and tourism) and to determine where monies should be channeled — for outside corporate interests or internal needs; developing social service agencies geared towards the culture of the community — language, mores, food, etc.; creating relevant education — education seen in a broad, historical context rather than as isolated incidents; having recreational programs for youth and adults which are run by the group for the group; and finally, having power to obtain what is necessary and desirable for the community on a nationwide basis. This last point requires involvement in the larger political arena and mobilizing for change by confronting the politicians and ruling class at the level of electoral politics and pressuring them on specific issues.

JOB DESCRIPTIONS

Staff Director: He/she will coordinate the overall activities of JCYC programs. He/she will hold weekly staff meetings with the program coordinators and other appropriate JCYC staff personnel. He/she will assign specific tasks to the staff (through the program coordinators) to be completed in accordance with a coordinated timetable and plan determined by himself/herself and the program coordinators, and approved by the Board of Directors. He/she will be responsible for the Ad Hoc programs (with the appropriate program coordinators or program heads). He/she will be responsible for the ESAP program through the ESAP-JCYC associate director. He/she will be responsible for the fiscal status of the organization through the fiscal agent and the finance workshop. He/she will be responsible for public relations either through a public relations workgroup or through a public relations coordinator. He/she will attend all Board of Directors meetings to serve as liason with the staff, provide information and resources to the Board and to advise the Board on any matters before it. He/she will be responsible for the completion of any directive from the Board of Directors to the staff. He/she will serve as chief liason between the Board and the staff.

Administrative Assitant: He/she will handle all correspondence, minutes and agendas, keep up files and records, and maintain the mailing list. He/she will be responsible for answering the business phone. He/she will work directly with the staff director in performing all necessary clerical duties and will coordinate all volunteer help in any of the above areas.

BUDGET AND RATIONALE:

Salaries:
Staff Director:

$300 per month for six months	$1800
Administrative Assistant:	
$300 per month for six months	1800
TOTAL	$3,600

Rationale: There are two points which have to be considered when viewing the request for salary funding: (1) the smallness of the salary; and (2) the equal amount of pay given to both positions.

It is the belief of the Japanese Community Youth Council that the capitalist ethic of striving for a high-paying job as the means to success places a great deal of emphasis on materialism. At JCYC, it is felt that work should be done because of the commitment one has for the goals of the organization. Money should not be the impetus for the type or amount of work that is done. For this reason, a salary should be given which is enough to survive on and which is required for workers who do not have any other form of income because of their work in JCYC.

Expanding further along this vein, commitment to work negates a higher status position demanding

69

more pay. This is an effort to break down the class basis which the larger society uses. This class basis inevitably develops into a ruling class and an oppressed class — the rich and the poor. Yet, the poor do not do less work in relation to the income they receive. They have been placed in poverty by those who do have the wealth and accompanying power. For these reasons, the pay is the same for both positions.

INCOME DURING 1971 CALENDAR YEAR

Third World Board, UC Berkeley	$ 942.64
Food Bazaar (Community festivals)	391.62
Film Rental	20.00
Donations	1,707.71
Daycamp/Children's Program Registrations	1,271.65
Nihonmachi Mini-Park Donations	1,367.16
TOTAL	**$5,700.78**

EXPENDITURES DURING THE
1971 CALENDAR YEAR

Programs:

Film Program (rental fees)	$ 42.64
Photography Workshop (chemicals, paper, film, etc.)	148.04
Ceramics Workshop (clay, glaze, etc.)	126.15
Arts and Crafts Workshop (paper, paints)	24.86
Silkscreen Workshop (silk, paper, film)	133.41
Draft Help (information leaflets, publicity, etc.)	131.25
Summer Daycamp/Fall Children's Program	1,376.62
Library (books, magazines, etc.)	148.34
SUBTOTAL	**$2,141.31**

Bills (garbage, utilities, insurance) $ 719.00

Administrative Operations (office supplies, subscriptions, finance records, etc.)   291.75

Recreation (gym rental, maintenance of equipment)   77.93

Public Relations (publicity, etc.)   48.00

Building Maintenance   418.78

Ad Hoc Projects (Community Services Day, Community Day, Nihonmachi Mini-Park)   791.72

SUBTOTAL	**$2,347.18**
TOTAL	**$4,488.49**

THE CENTER FOR RURAL STUDIES
FUNDING PROPOSAL FOR 1972/73

CONTENTS

73

PURPOSE

The Center is seeking funding to undertake various projects in 1972/73. The projects are action-oriented. Their objective is to promote a more equitable distribution of wealth and power in rural America.

SUMMARY

The Center for Rural Studies was founded in 1971 as a non-profit, tax-exempt public interest research group. It has been granted 501(c)(3) status by the Internal Revenue Service.

The Center is seeking $84,410 to finance its operations over the next twelve months. Among the projects the Center plans to undertake are:
- Development of a comprehensive land reform program for the United States;
- A national conference on land reform;
- An investigation of the agricultural subsidy program, with recommendations for restructuring it;
- A study of public land policy, with proposals for change;
- A study of railroad landholdings;
- A study of the impact of state and federal taxation on rural America, with recommendations for change.

THE PROBLEM

What can be done to alleviate rural poverty? What can be done to stem the outmigration from rural areas to already overcrowded cities? How can rural society be made more democratic, both economically and in terms of political power? How can the rural environment be protected against strip-mining, clear-cutting, excessive use of pesticides, and speculative land development? How can modern technology be managed so as to benefit, rather than dispossess, vast numbers of rural workers? How can people in rural areas regain control over their lives and livelihoods — control that is rapidly slipping away to corporate boardrooms in distant cities? How do federal and state policies, often unwittingly, contribute to the persistence of rural poverty, outmigration, social polarization, and environmental deterioration? How can these policies be changed? These are some of the major questions that the Center for Rural Studies intends to investigate and seek solutions to.

GOALS AND PHILOSOPHY

The goal of the Center for Rural Studies is to help make rural America economically and politically more democratic. It hopes to do this through research, educational activities, and litigation.

It is the philosophy of the Center that ownership of land by those who work and live on it is the key to alleviating rural poverty, easing urban overcrowding, reducing welfare costs and unemployment, protecting the rural environment, and building a stronger democracy.

Land and resources in rural areas are increasingly controlled by absentee corporations. Government encourages absentee corporate control through tax laws, subsidies, research and labor policies. These government policies should be changed. Rural economic development should be locally controlled, and the chief beneficiaries of government policies should be workers, not property owners.*

HISTORY OF THE CENTER FOR RURAL STUDIES

The Center was founded in 1971 by a number of people concerned about rural problems. Among those active in the formation of the Center were:

Sheldon Greene, general counsel of California Rural Legal Assistance; Geoffrey Faux, former director of economic development for the Office of Economic Opportunity and currently with the Center for Community Economic Development in Cambridge, Massachusetts; Berge Bulbulian, a small grape and raisin grower in Sanger, California; Robert Browne, director of the Black Economic Research Center and board member of the National Sharecroppers Fund; Peter Barnes, West Coast Editor of *The New Republic* and author of numerous articles dealing with rural America; Gerald Meral, scientific director of the Environmental Defense Fund; Polly Roberts, a member of the Ralph Nader Task Force on California Land Use; Roger Blobaum, economic consultant to the National Farmers Organization; Jim Hightower, director of the Agribusiness Accountability Project; David Talamonte, director of the Tri-County Economic Development Corporation, Modesto, California; Alfred Navarro, director of the Central Coast Counties Development Corporation, Aptos, California; Arthur Blaustein, associate director for Economic Development, National Housing and Economic Development Law Project; David Weiman, congressional intern to Senator Gaylord Nelson; Boren Chertkov, staff director, Senate Subcommittee on Migratory Labor; Dr.

*A fuller analysis of the Center's approach to rural problems is available upon request.

Paul Taylor, professor of economics emeritus, University of California, Berkeley; Michael Peevey, research director, California AFL-CIO; Jerry Berman, Center for Community Change; Charles Davenport, professor of law, University of California, Davis.

During 1971 and early 1972, many of the persons associated with the Center played active roles in studying and publicizing the problems of rural America. Research was and is being conducted on patterns of land ownership in California, New England, and the South; on railroad landholdings throughout the country; on the possibilities for land reform in the United States; on the enforcement of reclamation laws and the applicability of antitrust laws to agriculture; on the homestead and public land laws; and on the impact of tax laws on rural society. In several instances, presentations have been made to congressional committees and administrative commissions upon their request.

Activities of the Center *per se* have been limited in the past due to a lack of funds. All persons associated with the Center, with the exception of a single part-time secretary, have thus far donated their time and labor without remuneration. Printing, travel and secretarial costs have been met by small individual contributions.

STRUCTURE AND STAFFING OF THE CENTER

The activities of the Center are overseen by a board of directors that presently includes the following members:
- Peter Barnes;
- Robert S. Browne;
- Sheldon Greene;
- Arthur Blaustein;
- Robert Coles, M.D., research psychiatrist, Harvard University Health Services;
- Dorothy Bradley, state representative, Bozeman, Montana;

- John Stencel, president, Rocky Mountain Farmers Union;
- Rev. Shirley Greene, United Methodist Church, New York.

A special advisory board on tax policy includes:
- Prof. Charles Davenport;
- Prof. Donald Hagman, acting director, Institute for Government and Public Affairs, UCLA;
- William Bennett, member, California State Board of Equalization;
- Jonathon Rowe, Tax Reform Research Group, Washington, D.C.
- George Brown, former U.S. Congressman, Los Angeles;
- Prof. John Coons, University of California Law School, Berkeley.

The home base of the Center for Rural Studies is Berkeley, California. Regional affiliates are operative in Cambridge, Massachusetts, Washington, D.C., and Creston, Iowa.

Director and general counsel of the Center is Sheldon Greene. Peter Barnes is the co-director concerned with research and publications. Geoffrey Faux (New England), Roger Blobaum (Midwest) and James Hightower (Washington, D.C.) are regional coordinators. Regional affiliates will soon be established in Appalachia, the South and the Southwest.

Many of the persons associated with the Center are also associated with the National Coalition for Land Reform.

PROJECTS FOR 1972/73

If adequately funded, the Center will undertake the following projects in 1972/73:

− Development of a comprehensive land reform program. Elements of such a program might include regional public ownership of timber, coal and recreation land, and a federal land bank to purchase and resell or lease land to independent farmers and cooperatives.

78

— A national land reform conference. The purpose
of the conference will be twofold: to interchange information on landholding patterns in different re-
gions of the country, and to assist in developing the
land reform program mentioned above.

*— Investigation of the agricultural subsidy pro-
gram.* The crop subsidy program costs the public
nearly $10 billion annually. The bulk of the money
goes to large landowners, not to those who need it
most. The Center will recommend ways to restructure
the subsidy program so that it benefits working
farmers.

— Study of public land policies. More than a third
of the nation's land is still owned by the federal and
state governments. This land could be retained by the
public, given away to absentee corporations, or sold
or leased to local residents and cooperatives. Current
proposals for dispensing the public lands will be ana-
lyzed, and recommendations made.

— Study of railroad landholdings. During the nine-
teenth century, more than 150 million acres were
granted to private railroads by the federal and state
governments. The Center's study will explore the
present status of these lands, including more than 10
million acres still held by the railroads, and examine
the possibility of public re-acquisition.

— Study of federal and state tax policies. Tax policies such as the preferential treatment of capital gains
have a major impact on rural society. The Center,
guided by its tax advisory board and in consultation
with Accountants for the Public, a public interest accounting firm in San Francisco, will examine the impact of various tax policies and make recommendations for change.

— Administration of reclamation law. The Reclamation Act of 1902 provides that no single owner
shall receive federal irrigation for more than 160
acres, and that absentee owners shall receive no water

at all. This law has been poorly administered in the Western reclamation areas. The Center will investigate the administration of the Reclamation Act and make recommendations for change.

— *Litigation*. It is likely that causes for litigation will arise out of the Center's investigations. If so, the Center will assist in financing citizens' lawsuits aimed at remedying the illegalities uncovered.

—*News service*. The Center plans to establish a news service, directed towards interested persons, organizations, public officials and media. The purpose of the news service will be to disseminate information relevant to the movement for change in rural America.

FUNDING

The Center is essentially a public interest research group and as such has no regular source of income. Attempts have been made, and will continue to be made, to raise money from concerned individuals and organizations. However, in order for the Center to function effectively, the assurance of a minimum financial base is essential.

The Center will not be an overstaffed, overpaid bureaucracy. It will be a lean, flexible organization that at all times will maintain the lowest possible overhead. For foundations interested in promoting social change, the Center offers a way to achieve a relatively large impact with a relatively small financial investment.

CONCLUSION

The Center for Rural Studies is action-oriented. It hopes to make possible a more decent life for the millions of Americans of all races who live or want to live in rural areas. To accomplish its objectives it needs financial support from individuals and foundations. All contributions are tax-deductible.

APPENDICES*

Appendix A: Certification by Internal Revenue Service of 501 (c) (3) status

Appendix B: Letter of endorsement from Senator Adlai E. Stevenson III

Appendix C: "Land Reform in America" — reprint of articles by Peter Barnes, appearing in *The New Republic,* June 5, 12 and 19, 1971.

Appendix D: Resume of Sheldon Greene

Appendix E: Resume of Peter Barnes

---

*A copy of each of these documents was attached at the end of the original proposal.

BUDGET

The total annual budget for the Center is $84,410. This breaks down as follows:

Personnel

Director/general counsel	$ 6,500
Director/research/publications	6,500
Administrator/secretary	10,000
Regional coordinators:	
New England	2,000
Midwest	2,000
Washington, D.C.	2,000
Appalachia	2,000
South	2,000
Southwest	2,000
Student research	6,000
Consultants	4,000
SUBTOTAL	**$45,000**
Fringe Benefits (11%)	4,501
[excludes consultants]	
TOTAL	**$49,510**

Operating Expenses

San Francisco area headquarters:	
Rent	$ 2,400
Telephone	4,000
Printing/xeroxing	5,000
Books and periodicals	500
Travel (conferences, seminars)	9,000
Office supplies, postage	3,000
Regional offices (all expenses)	6,000
TOTAL	**$29,900**

Special Projects

Litigation Fund	5,000
GRAND TOTAL	**$84,410**

The above budget provides for implementation of the Center's proposed 1972/73 projects. The breakdown by project is as follows:

(1) Land reform project

Personnel conducting research	$10,500
Overhead	4,300
TOTAL	**$14,800**

(2) Land reform conference

Rental of conference facilities (includes room and food)	$ 2,500
Transportation of participants	5,000
Personnel	2,000
Overhead	1,000
TOTAL	**$10,500**

(3) Subsidy investigation

Personnel conducting research	$ 9,000
Overhead	3,000
TOTAL	**$12,000**

(4) Public land study

Personnel conducting research	$ 5,210
Overhead	2,500
TOTAL	**$ 7,710**

(5) Railroad landholding study

Personnel conducting research	$ 5,000
Overhead	2,000
TOTAL	**$ 7,000**

(6) Tax study

Personnel conducting research	$10,500
Overhead	2,500
TOTAL	**$13,000**

(7) Reclamation law study

Personnel conducting research	$ 3,100
Overhead	1,500
TOTAL	**$ 4,600**

(8) Litigation

Legal fees	4,000
Printing/xeroxing	1,000
TOTAL	**$ 5,000**

(9) News Service

Personnel	$ 4,200
Printing (based on 5,000 circulation and bi-monthly publication	3,000
Postage and addressograph	1,400
Overhead	1,200
TOTAL	**$ 9,800**
GRAND TOTAL	**$84,410**

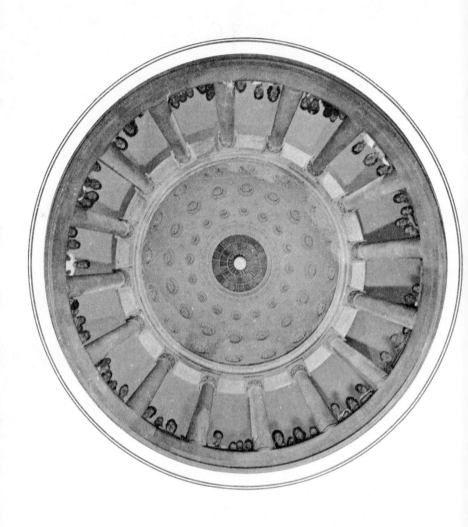

Visitors on a guided tour crowd the balustrade of the Senate Small Rotunda.

10

From the Ivory Tower:

A Bird's Eye View
from Within the Foundations

With high hopes—a proposal in hand—and a list of possible foundations in mind, you are ready to make contact with that potential source of funds—THE FOUNDATION. The long anxious waiting begins. How will the foundation respond? Will the proposal receive only a cursory glance and a routine reply, "not interested," or will it be studied and carefully evaluated by persons who have the ability to understand what you are attempting to do?

There are as many answers to this question as there are foundations. However, *The Bread Game* addresses itself primarily to groups engaged in social and institutional change.

A foundation executive laid the issue on the line when he said to such a group, "Write a description of your work which describes the many and varied aspects of the people and the community you are serving *without* including a single explicit or implied value judgment about the system with which you find yourselves in conflict." Simply stated, *leave out the rhetoric.* While those of us who serve foundations may be far removed from the problems, and many of us are a part of the system that created the problems, still it is counter-productive for you to bite the hand

85

that you hope will feed you. Trying to win foundation funding from the establishment, so that social change people can do their thing, is tough enough without intimidating or saying things that are more apt to start arguments."

This person identified the crisis and tension that exists between foundations who represent the establishment, and the community of persons who are seeking varying degrees of social change. Diatribes against the main stream of American society do little to bring persons together on a new level of understanding and communication. You can hardly expect a positive response from the foundations' side if they have been castigated and blamed for society's ills. This is not to say that the foundation world should not be confronted with its paternalistic role as a perpetuator of a system that pits the *haves* against the *have nots*. But how, when and where such confrontations take place must be considered carefully. If you choose your proposal as the instrument, then in all fairness you must be prepared to accept the consequences.

You're not going to be able to deal with unknowns such as political and social prejudices and persuasions, but there are objective criteria commonly used by foundations to evaluate proposals that should be considered:

1. **Who are the persons involved in the project, and what is their competence?** Are they the best of all possible people to undertake the venture? Are they persons known to members of the foundation, either staff or board? This is not essential, but it always helps. What is the opinion of the foundation person who reviewed the proposal? What kind of references were submitted with the proposal and how reliable are they?

2. **Next may come a close look at the feasibility and realism of the proposal.** Is the time right for such an endeavor? The answer to this question will most certainly depend on where the questioner is coming from. Uppermost in the minds of most foundations is whether the agency or institution involved is suitable for foundation support—meaning, are you a tax-exempt public charity with a 501(c)(3) from your friendly Internal Revenue Service? Is the sponsoring agency clearly enthusiastic about the proposal? There may be an examination of the proposed facilities and staff to determine if they are sufficient to do the job.

3. **Now for the nitty-gritty:** the foundation may examine the importance and utility of the project and its contribution to society. Is there a demonstrable need for the project? Whom will the project benefit and how? Will there be a measurable improvement if the venture is successful?

4. **A prime criterion for most foundations is originality and creativity.** Here the key word is "innovative"—but it is a word which should be used with extreme caution, if at all, in the written proposal. Is the project part of an already existing program? Does the project duplicate or overlap other existing or past programs? Could the project be better executed elsewhere or by other persons?

5. **Here comes the loaded one:** How appropriate is the project to the foundation's policy and current program focus? Is the program consistent with the foundation's current program objectives? If so, is it an area of priority?

6. **What are the project's "ripple effects?"** Will it produce a significant change in a wide

circle? Will the project attract other financial support? Will the results be transferrable to other projects and localities?

7. Is the foundation the only source of support? Are there public monies available, such as federal, state or local governments? Are there more appropriate private sources, such as other foundations, private institutions or individuals more active in the field of the proposal?

8 What about the budget? Is it sound? Is it generous enough, given the job to be accomplished, but not so generous as to be wasteful? Is the project director familiar with the administrative intricacies of conducting the proposed project, and are contingencies planned for?

9. How persistent and committed are the proponents? Have they devoted sufficient time to planning and launching the venture? What provision has been made for eventual self-support, or support from sources other than the foundation?

10. What provisions have been made for an objective evaluation of the results of this project? Will the project staff adequately record the successes and failures of the project? If the project lends itself to statistical evaluation, has provision been made for recording and analyzing relevant data? Where new programs are being developed, how will the information gained be reported to other communities?

These questions underscore the importance of doing your homework BEFORE you make your first contact with the **Ivory Tower Foundation.**

Researching Foundations -
Up from Under

From your side of the Ivory Tower, it is important to know some specifics in researching foundations: name and address, contact people, the best approach to a given foundation, waiting time for notification of funding and the foundation's own concerns and priorities. Sometimes the foundation's declared purpose and stated policy differ from its granting pattern. To note any discrepancies, you should check on previously-awarded grants.

As mentioned in Chapter 2, there are a number of different types of foundations. For example, *you should note if the agency is a community or private foundation.* The former more often provides enabling programs as well as money for projects; the latter usually provides only funding. When looking at a family-funded foundation, *find out the current interests of the donor family;* some fundraising consultants publish biographical sketches on decision-making trustees. You might also want to check out foundations in your local area; there are a number that specialize in helping community groups find appropriate means of support for their programs.

It is important to check on the proper approach to the foundation: How best can initial contact be made? Can a xeroxed proposal be submitted? Should other foundations be mentioned if the grant is submitted to more than one? May you contact trustees directly or should you go through prescribed .channels? Members of the foundation staff will know the answers to these questions. They screen proposals and make recommendations to the trustees or distribution committee. Cooperation with their way of doing things is critical, so don't be afraid to ask questions.

If you can afford professional fund-raising consultants you might want to consult the **Yellow Pages** for suggestions. Two that are nationally oriented are:

Lawson & Williams Foundation Research Service

Taft Information Services, Inc.
1000 Vermont Avenue, NW

Free brochures are available, but their services will range between $250 and $1,000 annually. Information is also available from **The Foundation Center**, a New York-based non-profit service agency for foundations and the public. It maintains regional information depositories in major cities, usually located at university libraries, that contain xeroxed or microfilmed copies of 990 AR annual reports from foundations to the Internal Revenue Service. Although the information is comprehensive, it is very often two to four years old. The Government requires foundations to file these annual reports with the IRS. Foundations must also publish a notice of availability in a local paper following the day of filing and must keep that report available at their central office for inspection for at least 180 days thereafter. While some foundations publish a comprehensive annual report which they distribute to the public, most foundations are not eager to publicize their general operations. A call will determine their policy on this. If they are cooperative, you can find out their current information on funding policies, priorities and grant-making procedures. *Again, don't be afraid to ask questions.*

11
Welcome to the Zoo:

Some Final Suggestions for
Your Foundation Trip

The Bread Game has attempted to define the nature of the foundation beast, the various species, and the general rules which apply to the chase. The rest is up to you.

Recall, if you will, our earlier description of the foundation beast and remember there are few beasts in our day and age who are able to roam the open country and adapt to the emerging environmental conditions of social change. Most of our beastie friends have been caged in a zoo with a specially treated, rarified atmosphere reminiscent of bygone days. We stand outside the cage in a world that has placed heavy demands upon us, forcing us to devise a plan of action by which we can enter the zoo and confront the beast in his lair.

Journey with us briefly through the zoo trip with an imaginary group known as People Against the System, Inc. PATSI is a grassroots group of people who have grown so fed up with the system that they have decided to organize a movement to simply eliminate the system entirely. "The system" included just about everything known to mankind.

In order to further its work, PATSI was going to need bread. So they secured a copy of *The Bread Game* and painstakingly began to implement its guidelines. Being an impatient lot, however, they skipped the first chapter dealing with the rules, for their only interest was finding the name, address, and telephone number of the foundation which would give them all the money they needed. Having discovered on page 16 that a book exists called *The Foundation Directory*, they ran to the local library and anxiously raced through the pages, looking for a list of foundations whose stated purpose was the elimination of the system. Much to their surprise, however, they could find no foundation which listed this as its criterion for making a grant. Undaunted, they raced through the *Grants Index* book to see if any foundation had made a grant to projects dealing with social change at all. The list was small indeed, but it *was* a list. PATSI took a new lease on life. But what was the next step?

There seemed to be nothing else to do but read the book—starting at the beginning.

Reading the section called "The Rules" was kind of trippy. "Foundations—Some Information You Need to Know"—dull, but helpful. "Third World Community"—kind of reassuring. But when they got to the chapter called "Formation of a Tax-Exempt Corporation" they were done in. How could an anti-establishment group buy that trip? Really—a board of directors, officers, minutes, annual meetings, reports ... this was going to be a heavy trip. But PATSI's leadership was undeterred. "If we don't do it," someone pointed out, "we ain't going to get no bread! Besides, who says bourgeois concepts of organization can't be given new meaning? Here we sit in a vacant store front with crates for furniture, a candle for light, wine for sustenance and people for action. Let's play the corporate game: everyone here is now PATSI's board of directors; who wants to be an officer?"

"This game isn't going to go anywhere unless we can find some mouthpiece who's gonna make us legal, and we don't have the bread for that trip."

"This book suggests we contact one of the legal aid societies. Supposedly they're set up to serve the people—and for free."

"Okay, get with it and contact them. In the meantime, that chapter called 'Sponsors' suggests some alternatives to getting incorporated.

"But would you believe this part about accounting? How can we commit ourselves to doing away with the system when at every turn we're being sucked into it by this kind of trip?"

"It's subject to *interpretation*. All they're saying is that we have to keep track of the bread we get and how we get rid of it."

"Man, I can't even keep track of the few bucks I get together for survival. How do you expect us to keep those kinds of records?"

"We don't have to do it all ourselves—we'll find some cat in the community who knows something about accounting to keep us on the straight and narrow."

"Hold it . . . hold it! Would you believe that they have suggested we should contact some of our wealthy friends and see if they won't give us some seed money?"

"The wealthiest friend I know is Jake who gets a monthly welfare check. So much for that trip."

"Maybe wealth is a relative question. . . . If Jake and all the other Jakes were to each give us a few coins, we could show some evidence for community support and maybe influence some rich dude to some in behind us too."

"Well, if that's all it takes, I guess we could raise a few bucks."

"Take a look at this section that calls for a written proposal. What a drag. I can't even spell my own name, much less put together our trip. I mean, I know what we're all about, but how are we going to convince somebody else if we have to follow all this crap?"

"Hey, man, you missed the point! They've given us a lot of information, but then they say the best way is to be ourselves and do the best we can. Maybe we can come up with something that honestly reflects where we are at and at the same time doesn't offend the senses of those foundation cats . . . you know, pick up on the positive. Like: 'People Against The System, Inc. requests of the No Such Foundation a grant of $15,000.00 to help all people discover human dignity and respect for themselves and their fellow human beings. Through a program of community education and action we will work to eliminate all elements in the community that tend to degrade, demoralize and otherwise make life untenable. PATSI has been at work for the past year and has already created a sense of community awareness for the task that is ahead.' In other words—we want to do away with the system. It's all subject to interpretation. . . ."

So PATSI is off and running with a difficult but not impossible task. The yellow brick path which leads to the zoo is circuitous and hazardous, but those who follow it will not be left entirely on their own. There are some zoo keepers and guides—friendly persons or organizations—along the way to point you in the right direction if you get turned around. Seek them out in your own community when you start.

May your search be fruitful!

94

12

Bibliography:

Where Else to Look

Andrews, F. Emerson. *"Applications for Grants,"* *Philanthropic Foundations.* New York: Russell Sage Foundation, 1956, pp. 170-194. $10.00
Order from: Order Services Department, Basic Books, Inc., P.O Box 4000, Scranton, Pennsylvania 18501.

Church, David M. *Seeking Foundation Funds.* New York: The National Public Relations Council of Health and Welfare Services, Inc., 419 Park Avenue South, New York, New York 10016.

Dermer, Joseph, ed. *How to Get Your Fair Share of Foundation Grants.* New York: Public Service Materials Center, 1973. 143 pp. $12.00.
Order from: Public Service Materials Center, 104 East 40th Street, New York, New York, 10016.

Dermer, Joseph. *How to Raise Funds from Foundations.* New York: Public Service Materials Center, 1972. 64 pp. $8.50.
Order from: Public Service Materials Center, 104 East 40th Street, New York, New York 10016.

Dermer, Joseph. *How to Write Successful Foundation Presentations.* New York: Public Service Materials Center, 1972. 80 pp. $8.95.
Order from: Public Service Materials Center, 104 East 40th Street, New York, New York 10016.

Hill, William J. *A Comprehensive Guide to Successful Grantsmanship.* Littleton, Colorado: Grant Development Institute, 1972. Looseleaf. $24.00
Order from: The Grant Development Institute, 2552 Ridge Road, Littleton, Colorado 80120.

Knittle, Fred D. *How to Obtain Foundation Grants.* Los Angeles: R. L. Houts Associates, Inc., 1972. 345 pp. $75.00
Order from: R. L. Houts Associates, Inc., 3960 Wilshire Boulevard, Los Angeles, California 90010.

MacIntyre, Michael. *How to Write a Proposal.* Washington, D.C.: Education, Training, and Research Sciences Corp., 1971. 55 pp. $3.95.
Order from: Volt Information Sciences, Inc., 1828 L Street, N.W., Room 1107, Washington, D.C. 20036.

Mirkin, Howard R. *The Complete Fund Raising Guide.* New York: Public Service Materials Center, 1972. 159 pp. $12.50.
Order from: Public Service Materials Center, 104 East 40th Street, New York, New York 10016.

Urgo, Louis A. and Robert J. Corcoran. *A Manual for Obtaining Foundation Grants.* Boston: Robert J. Corcoran Company, 1971. 14 pp. $5.75.
Order from: Robert J. Corcoran Company, 40 Court Street, Boston, Massachusetts 02108.